WHAT'S INSIDE?

Welcome to another Totally Inappropriate coloring book, the original cheekily profane (yet positive) adult coloring book series. Check out a few of the 35 gorgeous, inspiring designs in this book, just waiting for you to color them:

LET'S GET COLORING!

The Totally Inappropriate Coloring Books:

YOU'RE THE SHIT
YOU'RE TOTALLY BADASS
YOU ARE ONE BAMF
F♥CK CANCER*

*(a portion of the proceeds donated to research dedicated to finding a cure for cancer)

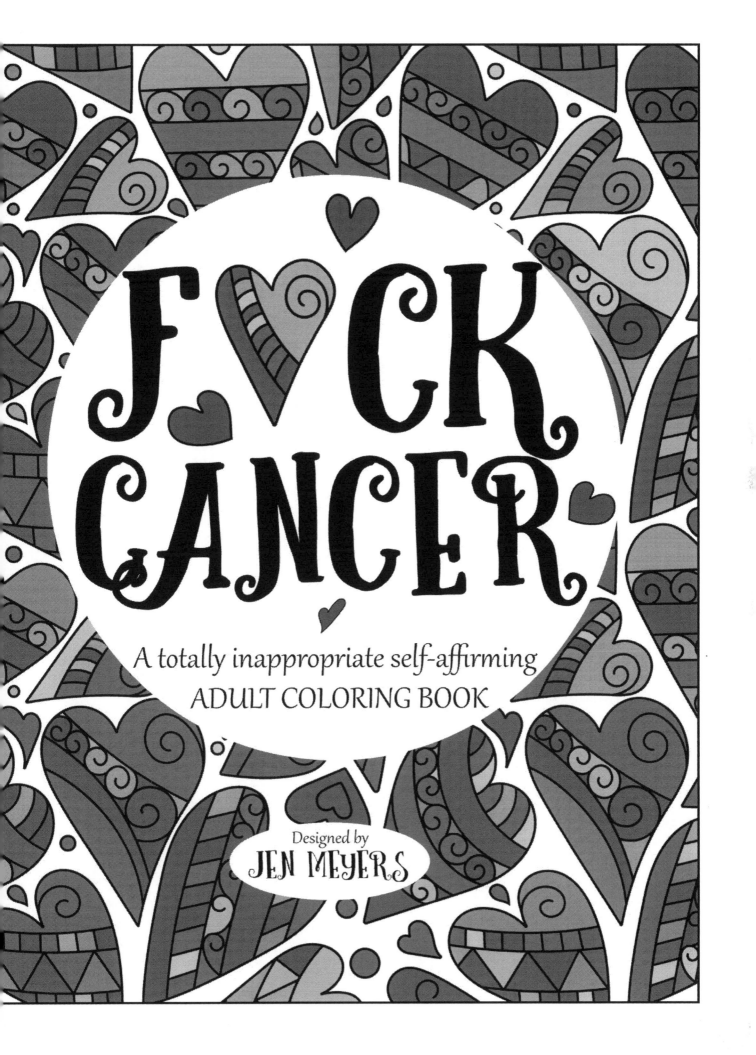

Please Note: This books contains adult language
and is not intended for children.

Published in June 2017 by Turning Leaves Press, Inc.

ISBN 978-1548184506

WELCOME!

Has cancer affected your life? Chances are it has—it certainly has mine.

In 2013, my brother died after a 15-year battle with a rare, incurable cancer. He was 46 years old, and I cannot tell you how many times I uttered the phrase "fuck cancer" while he was fighting it.

I still do. On a very regular basis.

John fought hard, with grace and a seemingly unlimited supply of positivity that I am still in awe of to this day. He was in incredible pain for all those years, but rarely complained or wallowed in self pity. Accepting what he could not change (his favorite phrase was "It is what it is"), he made the best of each moment. He was grateful for every day that he lived, and stockpiled memories with his wife and kids, friends and family, touching lives in ways I never realized until after he was gone.

My brother was a total badass in how he handled living with cancer.

This book is for him.

And this book is for *you*. If you are fighting cancer, this is for you. If your brother, sister, mom, dad, son, daughter, relative, or friend is fighting cancer, this is for you. If you've lost someone to cancer like I have, this is for you. If cancer affects your life in any way, this for you.

The stress of cancer—whether you or someone you love is facing it—is immense. And if this coloring book can bring a little relief, hopefully a smile, and perhaps even a boost to your inner resolve to fight harder, to keep going even when you're tired, hurting, and don't think you can, then it will be doing exactly what I hoped it would. For you.

You are worth it. You are not alone. You are a total badass.

And I believe in you.

You've got this.

Inappropriately yours,

JEN

P.S. A portion of the profits from this book will be donated to support research dedicated to finding a cure for cancer. Because fuck cancer.

Think positive

obviously never had cancer

whoever said winning isn't everything

Never give up

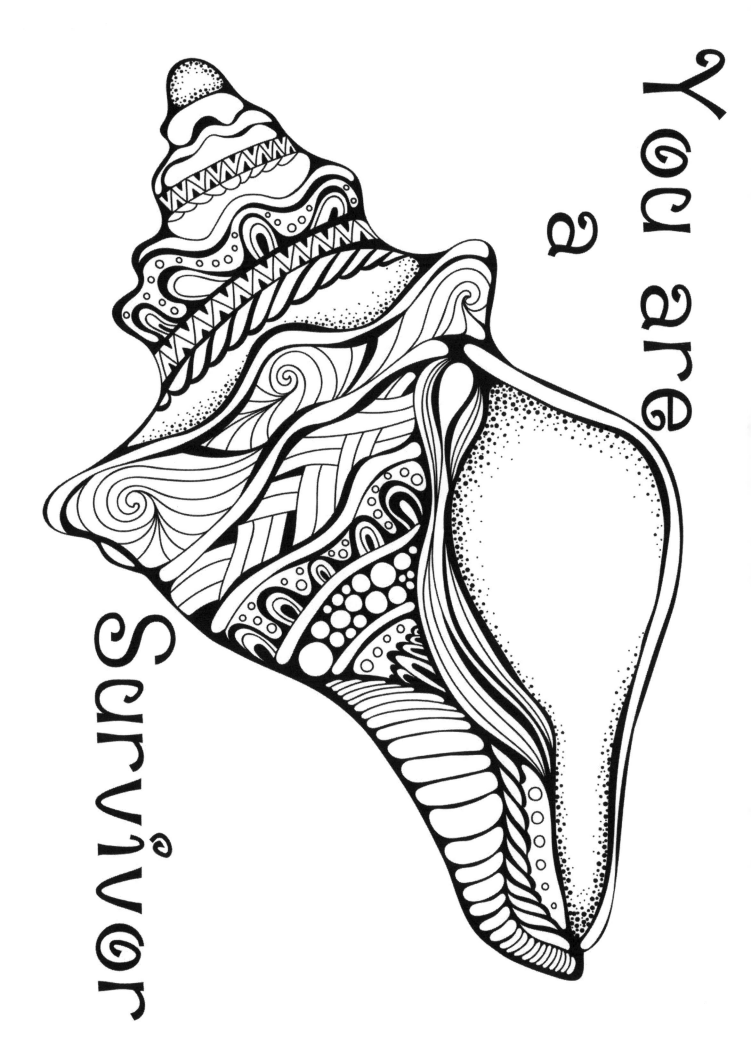

You are a Survivor

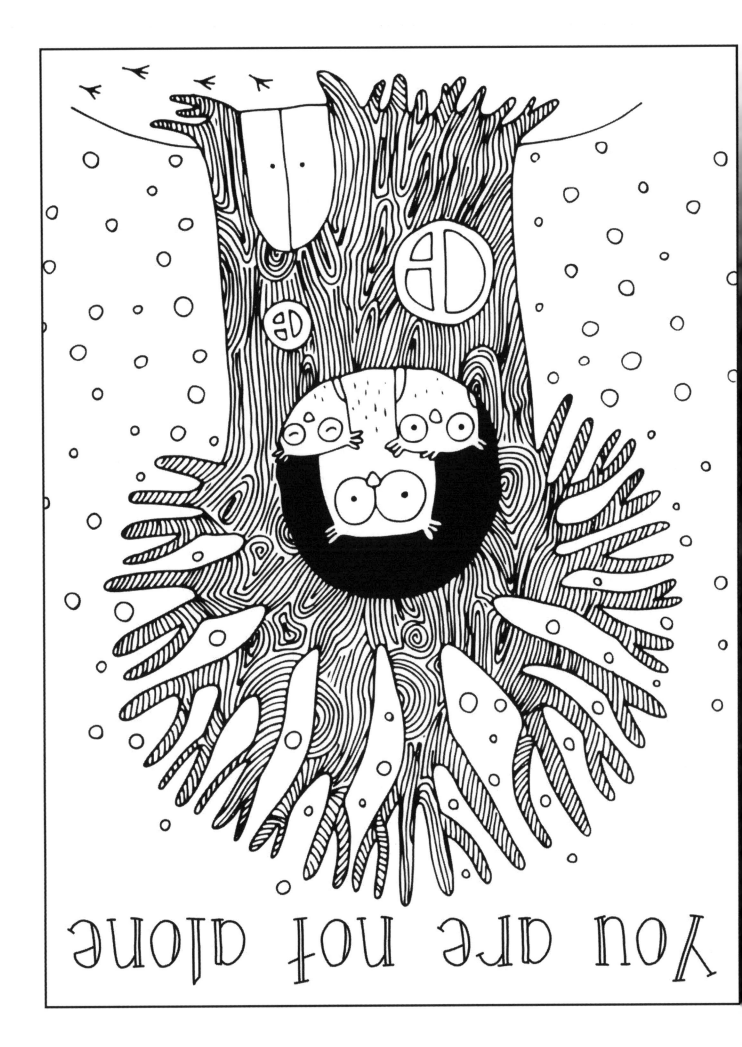

Fight like the badass you are.

Even the most delicate among us
can be a BADASS
when they have to.

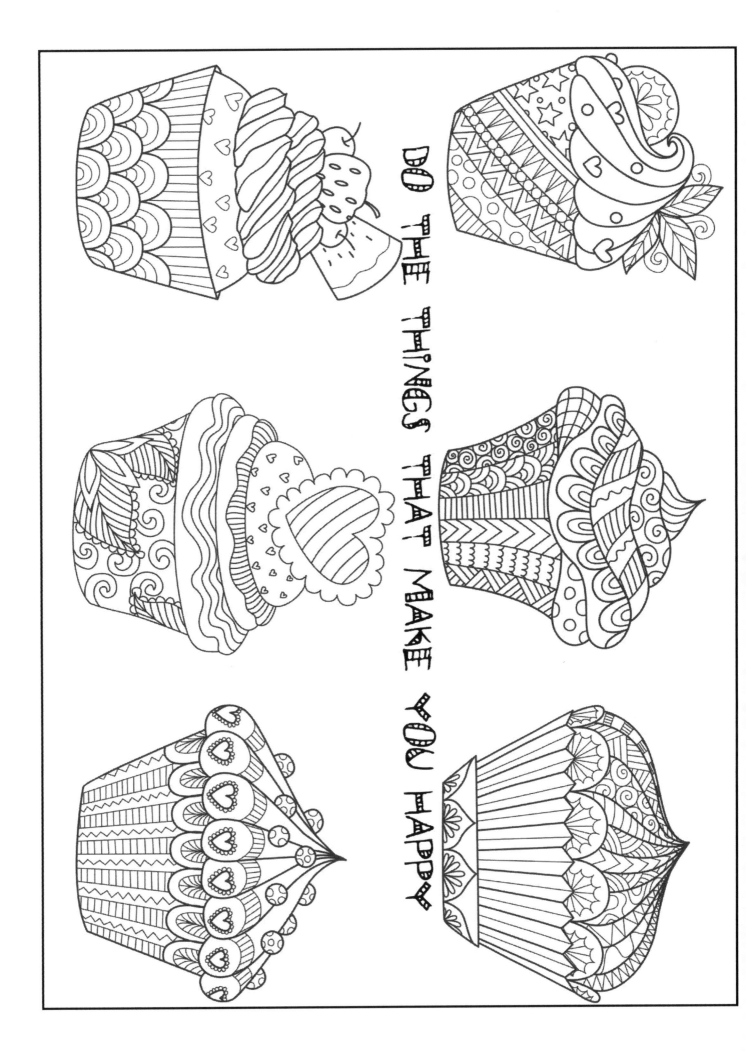

live the shit out of this day.

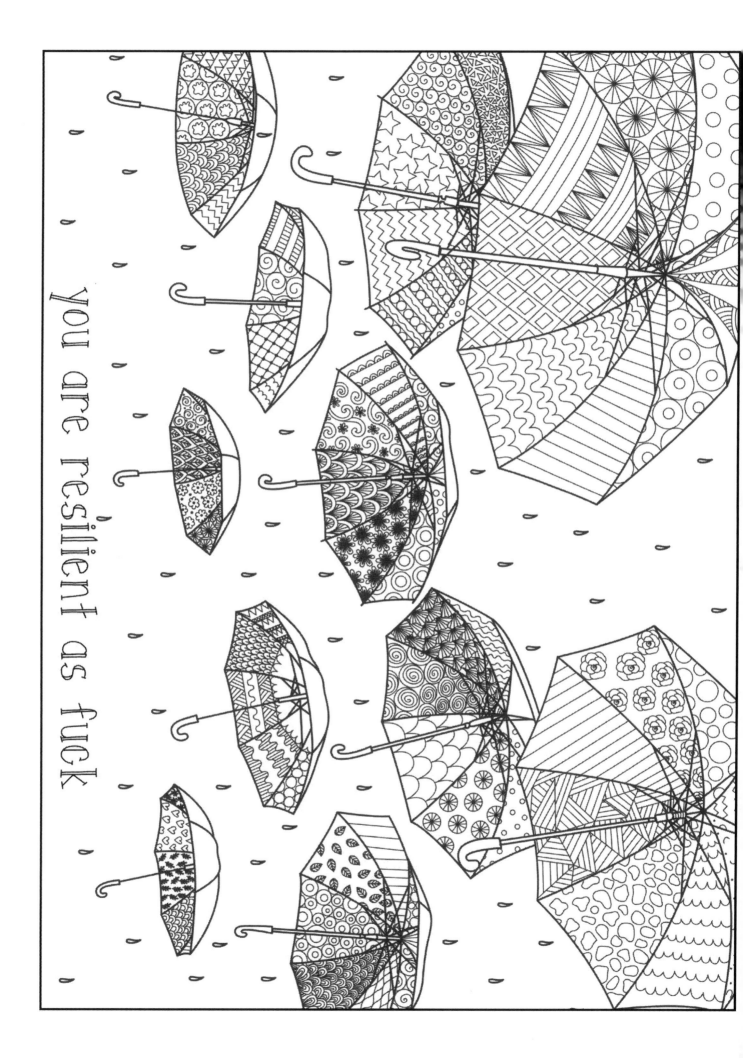

Thank You!

I truly hope this coloring book brought you joy—that's why I created it. I'd love to hear from you. Drop me a line at jen@jmeyersbooks.com or visit me on Facebook at www.facebook.com/jmeyersbooks. I'm also on Twitter and Instagram as @jmeyersbooks.

Warmly,
JEN

JEN MEYERS grew up in Vermont, spent three years in Germany when she was a kid, and now lives in central New York. When she's not reading, writing, or designing coloring books, she's chasing after her four kids, playing outside, relishing the few quiet moments she gets with her husband, and forgetting to make dinner.

Besides designing Totally Inappropriate coloring books, she also writes contemporary romance and young adult fantasy. She is the author of the (completely appropriate) *Intangible* series, the (perfectly inappropriate) *Happily Ever After* series and *Anywhere*, and co-author of the (totally inappropriate) *Untamed* series. For more information about Jen and her work, visit her website www.jmeyersbooks.com.

62668740R00044